J   4959
226.7
C

Caswell, Helen

Loves & fishes

Loaves & Fishes

WRITTEN AND ILLUSTRATED BY
Helen Caswell

Abingdon Press
NASHVILLE

Library of Congress Cataloging-in-Publication Data

Caswell, Helen Rayburn.
   Loaves and fishes/Helen Caswell.
      p.   cm.
   Summary: Retells the familiar Bible story from the point of view of young Thomas,
who offers his own lunch of five little barley loaves and two fish to Jesus, who in turn
uses them to feed a crowd of thousands.
   ISBN 0-687-22526-4 (pbk.:alk. paper)   1. Feeding of the five thousand
(Miracle)—Juvenile literature.   2. Bible stories, English—N.T. Gospels.   [1. Feeding of
the five thousand (Miracle)   2. Jesus Christ—Miracles   3. Bible stories—N.T.]   I. Title.
BT367.F4C37   1993
226.7'09505—dc20   93-25308

Printed in Singapore

Thomas was going fishing. Although he was a
little boy, his mother let him go off fishing by himself
because he was always careful, and he *almost* always brought
back some fish for their supper. She wrapped up five little barley loaves
for his lunch, and waved to him as he went off, whistling.

Thomas had a favorite fishing hole that only he knew about. The water was very safe and shallow except for one place that was a bit deeper, where the fish liked to come. It was very quiet and peaceful, which was one reason it was such a good fishing place. The fish didn't come close to the shore if there were lots of people and noise.

He sat patiently holding his fishing pole for quite a long time. Finally, he felt the pole jerk, and there was a fish! Then he caught another one! He felt lucky. He decided he would cook the two fish for his lunch. They would taste good with his barley loaves, and he could catch more later to take home to his mother.

Thomas carefully started a little fire on the beach, and put his fish on a willow stick to cook. They were just getting brown, and smelled wonderful, when Thomas heard the sound of voices.

Far down the shore was a crowd of people hurrying toward him. Thomas could hardly believe it. Nobody ever came to this lonely spot! Why now? And why so many? As they came closer he heard what they were shouting: "There he comes! See the boat? But we knew where he was headed, and we got here first!"

Then Thomas looked out across the water and saw the boat with some men in it, coming close to the shore. He recognized one of the men. His name was Jesus, and everyone was talking about him because he had cured many sick people. Wherever Jesus went, crowds followed him. He looked very tired, and Thomas thought he knew why Jesus had come to this lonely spot. He wanted some peace and quiet.

But the crowd had followed him, and there would be no peace and quiet now. The fish would all be frightened away, too. Thomas was disgusted. He wouldn't be able to catch any more fish for his mother. Well, he'd just take her the two he'd cooked for his lunch. Quickly he wrapped them up with the barley loaves.

Jesus and his friends got out of the boat and greeted the noisy crowd on the beach. Jesus' friends were called disciples, Thomas remembered. They looked cross, seeing the thousands of people. But Jesus smiled and began to talk to the people, answering their questions, telling them stories, and making them feel better. Thomas could hardly take his eyes off Jesus' face—so kind and loving, even though Thomas *knew* Jesus was so tired and really wanted to be alone for a little while.

Before he knew it, the sky was turning a purplish color, and Thomas realized that it was almost suppertime. How fast the time had gone!

One of the disciples said, "This is a lonely place, and the time has slipped by; so send the people away, and they can go to the villages to buy themselves some food."

Jesus said, "There is no need for them to go; give them something to eat yourselves."

The disciples looked at one another, wide-eyed. Thomas saw that they had no food to give the people, and before he even thought about it, he unwrapped his five little barley loaves and the two fish and said, "Here. You can have these!"

The men began to laugh, and then Thomas looked at the crowd of thousands of people and he turned red with embarrassment. How silly he'd been! His little loaves and fishes wouldn't even start to feed so many people!

But Jesus thanked him, smiling solemnly. He took the five little loaves and the two little fishes, and holding them in his hands, he looked up to heaven and said the blessing.

Then, while Thomas's eyes got bigger and bigger, Jesus began breaking the

loaves and fishes into
pieces, and handing the
pieces to his disciples to
give to the crowd of people.
The men had stopped
laughing. Nobody was
laughing, as the thousands
of people sat down in rows
in the tall grass, and the
disciples handed out the food.

Thomas watched Jesus' hands as they kept breaking off pieces of the loaves and the fishes—enough pieces to feed the thousands of people all they could eat, and Thomas's little loaves and the two little fishes never got any smaller.

At last Jesus said to his disciples, "Pick up the pieces left over, so that nothing gets wasted."

The disciples gathered up all that was left and filled twelve baskets with the scraps. Thomas wrapped up as much as he could, to take home to his mother.

Thomas had been too amazed to eat, but now at last he
ate his two fish and some of the little loaves. He didn't
know if they were the same fish he'd caught and the same
loaves his mother had given him or what. It was confusing
if you thought about it. But they tasted good, and he was hungry.

He looked up at Jesus and Jesus smiled at him, and Thomas
smiled back.

Then, before the crowd noticed, Jesus walked quietly away into the hills. People started crying out, "Where's Jesus? Where did he go?"

Thomas didn't tell them. Jesus deserved a little peace and quiet.